Jetson Orin Nano Super:

TRANSFORMING EDGE AI WITH NVIDIA'S GAME-CHANGING SUPERCHIP"

"A Deep Dive into Its Power, Efficiency, and Groundbreaking Influence"

Linden L. Sommerfeld

Table of Content

Introduction

The world is on the cusp of a technological revolution, where intelligence is no longer confined to massive data centers or cloud servers far from reach. Instead, it's becoming more personal, embedded in the devices we use everyday—smaller, quicker, and more powerful than we ever imagined.

This shift is more than a tale of hardware; it's about a quiet transformation reshaping how machines think, learn, and interact with the world. And leading this charge is NVIDIA's Jetson Orin Nano Super, a device destined to challenge the limits of what we believe is possible at the intersection of AI and edge computing.

Envision a device compact enough to power autonomous machines, capable of navigating unknown environments, analyzing massive data in real-time, and making decisions faster than any human could. Picture a future where industries like healthcare, robotics, and smart cities are powered by devices that do more than just crunch numbers—they truly understand their surroundings. This is no longer a distant vision from a science fiction story; it's happening now, with the Jetson Orin Nano Super leading the way.

But this isn't just about tech specs and performance figures. The real story lies in its ability to bridge the gap between human creativity and machine intelligence. It represents a world where edge AI serves as an equalizer, giving startups, researchers, and creators the freedom to transform their ideas without the barriers of cost or complexity. What used to require immense computing power now fits in the palm of your hand, thanks to this remarkable technology.

This book takes you on an exploration of the Jetson Orin Nano Super—its capabilities, its applications, and the innovations it's sparking. From autonomous robots to groundbreaking healthcare solutions, you'll discover how this device is changing industries and empowering visionaries to make breakthroughs we're only beginning to understand. This is not just technology advancing; it's technology accelerating toward a smarter, more interconnected future.

The Jetson Orin Nano Super is more than a hardware device. It's a window into the future of humanity's relationship with technology, where small devices make massive impacts, and edge AI opens up entirely new realms of possibility. So, let's dive in and explore this thrilling world of Super AI.

Chapter 1: The Rise of Artificial Intelligence at the Edge

Artificial intelligence (AI) has fundamentally transformed the way we interact with technology, sparking a shift in industries and revolutionizing innovation. At the core of this transformation is the concept of Edge AI—an innovation that allows machines to process data and make decisions locally, right where the data is created.

This new approach eliminates the need to send data to distant servers or the cloud, unlocking a whole new level of possibilities. To truly understand the significance of Edge

AI, we must first take a closer look at its foundational elements and how it fits into the broader landscape of modern computing.

What Exactly is Edge AI?

In simple terms, Edge AI represents the combination of artificial intelligence and edge computing. Instead of relying on far-off servers to analyze data, Edge AI enabled devices like cameras, sensors, and autonomous machines to process data directly where it's generated. This means decisions are made in real time, at the point of action, without waiting for data to travel to the cloud for analysis. This innovation reduces latency and enhances privacy, efficiency, and reliability.

Take, for example, a self-driving car. In the past, it would need to send data to a central server, wait for analysis, and then receive instructions. With Edge AI, however, the car can immediately interpret its environment, make decisions, and navigate safely in real time. Edge AI empowers devices to think and act swiftly, right on the spot.

Comparing this to traditional cloud computing, where data is processed remotely, highlights just how significant the shift is. Cloud computing relies on constant connectivity and data transfer, leading to potential delays—latency—especially in critical fields like healthcare, robotics, and autonomous vehicles, where every millisecond matters. Edge AI, on the other hand, brings the intelligence closer to the action, making decisions instantly and reducing reliance on external networks. It's not about replacing the cloud, but rather complementing it, creating a hybrid system that maximizes both local and remote computing.

The Journey Through AI Hardware: A Story of Progress

The rise of Edge AI didn't happen overnight. It's part of a much longer journey in the evolution of AI hardware, one that has been marked by relentless innovation. Initially, central processing units (CPUs) were the primary workhorses of early computing. While they were versatile, they weren't optimized to handle the immense demands of AI algorithms.

As AI grew more complex, Graphics Processing Units (GPUs) entered the scene. GPUs, originally designed for rendering graphics, were much better suited for parallel processing, which made them ideal for training and running AI models. NVIDIA, a leader in GPU technology, quickly recognized the potential of GPUs to transform the landscape of AI. With their CUDA platform, NVIDIA allowed developers to harness GPUs for demanding computations, leading to the explosion of deep learning in the 2010s.

However, as AI applications continued to grow, the need for more specialized hardware arose. This led to the development of Application-Specific Integrated Circuits (ASICs) and Tensor Processing Units

(TPUs), which were purpose-built to handle the specific needs of AI tasks. These advances made significant strides, but they presented new challenges—especially in terms of scaling AI to edge devices, which are much smaller, more compact, and require energy efficiency.

The Emergence of the Jetson Orin Nano Super: Bridging the Gap

This brings us to the Jetson Orin Nano Super, a product that marks the next step in the evolution of AI hardware. It brings together decades of technological advancements, culminating in a device designed to empower the next wave of AI at the edge. NVIDIA has played a pivotal role in democratizing AI, not just by making GPUs accessible to researchers but by creating platforms like the Jetson series, which enable edge computing without compromising on performance.

The Jetson Orin Nano Super is a powerful, compact solution that combines the high performance needed for complex AI tasks with energy efficiency, making it suitable for edge devices like autonomous drones, robots, and smart cameras. Its Ampere architecture—with 512 CUDA cores and 16 Tensor Cores—gives it the capability to perform up to 40 trillion operations per second. That's immense computing power packed into a small form factor that fits in the palm of your hand.

But what truly sets the Jetson Orin Nano Super apart is its versatility. It's not just about raw power—it's about enabling real-world, practical applications. Whether it's autonomous vehicles navigating city streets or drones monitoring environmental conditions, this chip makes it all possible. It's a glimpse into a future where AI isn't confined to massive, costly data centers but is distributed to where it's needed most—on the edge.

Chapter 2: The Unveiling of the Jetson Orin Nano Super

A New Era in Edge AI

In the fast-paced world of technology, progress is often defined by breakthroughs that push the boundaries of what's possible. Enter the Jetson Orin Nano Super—a breakthrough that redefines edge AI computing. This compact yet powerful superchip isn't just an incremental improvement; it's a leap forward, bringing cutting-edge AI performance to devices designed for real-world applications. To truly understand what makes this device so special, we need to dive deeper into its inner workings, explore the elements that make it "super," and see how it's poised to revolutionize the world of edge AI.

Inside the Superchip: The Heart of Innovation

At the core of the Jetson Orin Nano Super lies NVIDIA's Ampere architecture, a powerful platform that delivers exceptional AI processing performance in a small, energy-efficient form. This superchip features 512 CUDA cores and 16 Tensor Cores, enabling it to execute a staggering 40 trillion operations per second. Such immense computational power makes it ideal for real-time AI tasks, from decision-making in robotics to smart city applications.

With the Jetson Orin Nano Super, NVIDIA has packed the raw performance of a data-center GPU into a portable device that fits in the palm of your hand. But the magic doesn't stop with raw power—this chip is designed to be efficient, meaning it can run demanding AI workloads while consuming minimal energy. Available with either 4GB or 8GB of LPDDR5 RAM, the Orin Nano Super ensures there's enough memory bandwidth to handle the most data-intensive applications.

Compared to earlier models like the Jetson Nano and Jetson Xavier NX, the Jetson Orin Nano Super represents an enormous leap forward. For example, the original Jetson Nano delivered 472 GFLOPS, which was impressive for its time but pales in comparison to the Orin Nano Super's 40 TOPS (Tera Operations Per Second). This incredible leap in processing power is what sets the Orin Nano Super apart from its predecessors and makes it an indispensable tool for developers and innovators.

The "Super" Factor: What Makes This Chip Truly Exceptional

The term "Super" in Jetson Orin Nano Super isn't just a name—it's a promise. This chip is designed to deliver the ultimate balance of performance, energy efficiency, and adaptability. Let's break down what makes it stand out.

First, let's talk about future scalability. While the Jetson Orin Nano Super is already a powerhouse, NVIDIA is designing the chip with room to grow. Imagine a future version that features expanded memory configurations, allowing it to handle even larger AI models or manage multiple tasks simultaneously. Even more exciting is the possibility of dual GPU configurations, which would allow the chip to perform parallel processing on a scale once reserved for high-end servers. This would push the boundaries of what edge devices can achieve, taking Edge AI to new heights.

Another key factor that sets the Jetson Orin Nano Super apart is its power efficiency. Despite its incredible performance, the device operates within a modest power range of just 7 to 15 watts, making it ideal for applications where energy consumption is critical—think drones, mobile robots, or portable medical devices. With the Jetson Orin Nano Super, NVIDIA has created a chip that delivers both top-tier performance and energy-conscious operation, opening up new possibilities for mobile, battery-powered devices.

How the Jetson Orin Nano Super Works: Bridging AI Models and Real-World Applications

The Jetson Orin Nano Super is much more than just a chip; it's a complete AI platform that brings powerful edge computing capabilities to life. To understand how this device works, it's important to look at the entire process, from AI model training to deployment.

Typically, AI models are developed on powerful servers with access to vast amounts of data. These models are trained to recognize patterns, make predictions, and process large datasets. This training process requires significant computational power, which is where GPUs and TPUs come into play. Once the model is trained, the challenge becomes deploying it in real-world environments where it can make decisions and take actions based on new, incoming data. This is where the Jetson Orin Nano Super excels.

The process starts with training, where an AI model is created and optimized using huge datasets. For instance, an AI model could be trained to recognize objects in images or to interpret data from sensors in autonomous vehicles. Once the model is trained, it's ready for deployment, where it is used in real-time applications.

The Jetson Orin Nano Super is designed to handle this deployment phase with ease. By using Tensor Cores, which are specialized processing units optimized for matrix calculations, the chip can run AI inference—the process of making predictions based on new data—instantly and efficiently. Whether it's a robot navigating a complex environment or a smart camera analyzing video footage for potential security threats, the Jetson Orin

Nano Super can process data on-site, without the need for cloud-based analysis.

One of the standout features of the Jetson Orin Nano Super is its software ecosystem. NVIDIA's JetPack SDK is a comprehensive toolkit that developers can use to create and optimize AI applications for the Jetson platform. From deep learning libraries to computer vision tools, JetPack provides everything needed to deploy AI applications quickly and easily. In addition, the Jetson Orin Nano Super supports TensorRT, NVIDIA's high-performance deep learning inference library, which helps optimize AI models to run efficiently on the device, reducing latency and improving throughput.

The Jetson Orin Nano Super as a Complete Solution

At the end of the day, the Jetson Orin Nano Super is not just about the hardware—it's about providing a holistic solution for Edge AI developers. The combination of powerful hardware, efficient processing, and a robust software platform makes it an ideal choice for anyone looking to bring AI to the edge. Whether you're building a smart camera for a security system, an autonomous robot for industrial applications, or a medical device for real-time health monitoring, the Jetson Orin Nano Super is the device that makes it all possible.

Chapter 3: Real-World Wonders

How the Jetson Orin Nano Super is Transforming Industries

We are living in a time when artificial intelligence is no longer confined to cloud servers or experimental labs—it's in our streets, our homes, our hospitals, and our factories. And leading this technological migration from the cloud to the real world is NVIDIA's Jetson Orin Nano Super.

This tiny yet mighty chip has become the heartbeat of a revolution, driving intelligent machines and systems that can think, act, and adapt in real time. In this chapter, we explore the vibrant tapestry of real-world use cases that demonstrate how this "superchip" is quietly reshaping our everyday experiences.

Smarter, Faster, Autonomous – The New Face of Robotics

Few sectors have embraced AI as passionately as robotics. And now, with the Jetson Orin Nano Super in the mix, robots are evolving from rule-following machines into independent thinkers. In factories, for instance, robotic arms powered by the Orin Nano Super are no longer just repeating tasks—they're inspecting products, spotting flaws, optimizing assembly lines, and even learning to work alongside humans in shared environments.

Out in the fields, agricultural robots are taking farming to a new level. Drones equipped with this superchip fly over acres of crops, using onboard vision and AI models to detect pest infestations, nutrient deficiencies, or areas needing irrigation—all in real time. Ground-based bots are using the same tech to automate tasks like planting, harvesting, and monitoring soil health. These aren't science fiction fantasies; they're operational today, increasing yield and sustainability.

And in healthcare, robotic assistants are performing intricate surgeries with extraordinary precision. Thanks to the Jetson Orin Nano Super, these systems can process patient data on the spot, provide feedback to surgeons, and make real-time adjustments. Autonomous delivery robots are also roaming hospital corridors, safely transporting medical supplies, reducing staff workload, and boosting efficiency in care delivery.

Cities That Think – Smarter Urban Spaces and IoT Networks

Our cities are evolving into living, breathing ecosystems powered by data—and at the center of this transformation is edge computing. Smart city solutions driven by the Jetson Orin Nano Super are enabling real-time responses to everything from traffic jams to environmental hazards.

Take traffic management. Traditional systems use fixed schedules and limited data points, leading to bottlenecks and inefficiencies. With the Orin Nano Super embedded in traffic cameras and street sensors, cities can now analyze traffic patterns on the fly. Lights adjust based on real-time flow, reducing congestion and emissions. Accidents can be detected immediately, and alternate routes can be suggested—all without relying on cloud connectivity.

Environmental monitoring has also become hyperlocal and responsive. Sensors placed throughout cities collect air quality, temperature, humidity, and noise data. The Orin Nano Super processes this information on-site, alerting officials when pollution spikes or triggering warnings during extreme weather events. This not only improves public health but also makes cities more resilient to climate challenges.

One unsung hero powered by this superchip is predictive infrastructure maintenance. Bridges, power grids, and public transport systems outfitted with smart sensors can now self-diagnose potential failures. Instead of waiting for breakdowns, cities can act proactively, saving costs, reducing downtime, and preventing disasters.

Revolutionizing Healthcare with AI at the Patient's Side

Healthcare is entering a golden age of AI-assisted precision—and edge AI is playing a starring role. The Jetson Orin

Nano Super brings medical-grade AI to places where decisions need to be made fast: inside hospitals, at the patient's bedside, and even in remote rural clinics.

One of the most data-intensive tasks in medicine is imaging. MRI, X-ray, and CT machines produce enormous volumes of data, traditionally analyzed offsite, sometimes with long delays. Now, imaging devices powered by the Orin Nano Super can analyze scans in seconds, delivering instant results to doctors. This real-time diagnosis enables quicker, more accurate decisions—and often, better outcomes.

Then there's the rise of smart wearables. Devices that once just tracked heart rate are now mini diagnostic labs. With the Jetson

Orin Nano Super under the hood, wearables can identify irregular rhythms, detect early signs of disease, and even alert users or caregivers before emergencies arise.

Edge AI also powers advanced diagnostic platforms, capable of integrating data from multiple sources—electronic medical records, genetic profiles, lab tests—and identifying health risks earlier than ever before. In managing infectious diseases, for example, these systems help trace outbreaks, optimize resource allocation, and personalize treatments—all with data processed locally for speed and security.

Retail Intelligence and Next-Gen Surveillance

Step into a modern retail store, and you might not realize that you're walking into a data-rich, AI-enhanced environment—many of them powered by the Jetson Orin Nano Super. Retailers are using edge AI to turn every aisle and display into a source of insight.

Smart cameras track customer movement and behavior—not in a creepy way, but to understand flow patterns, dwell time, and purchasing tendencies. This helps stores redesign layouts, improve customer experience, and even tailor promotions based on live behavior. Inventory shelves monitor themselves, alerting staff when items are running low or restocked incorrectly. Some stores use these systems to personalize digital signage in real time.

Security has also taken a giant leap forward. Instead of relying on humans to monitor endless video feeds, AI-powered surveillance systems now detect suspicious behavior, recognize faces or license plates, and flag anomalies instantly. The Orin Nano Super's real-time processing ensures these systems don't just record—they react.

And beyond security, this tech is being used in crowd control and event management, helping authorities monitor crowd density, spot potential safety concerns, and even control access to restricted areas.

Chapter 4: Why the Edge is Epic

Unlocking the Power of the Jetson Orin Nano Super

The Jetson Orin Nano Super isn't just an impressive piece of technology—it represents a fundamental shift in how we think about artificial intelligence. In this chapter, we peel back the layers to reveal why this compact superchip isn't just useful—it's revolutionary. It's about much more than faster computations or smaller devices. It's about redefining where, how, and by whom intelligent systems are built and deployed. From speed and scale to cost and access, the Jetson Orin Nano Super is changing the game.

Scaling Smarts: Efficiency Without Delay

In the world of edge AI, speed is survival. The longer a machine waits to make a decision, the more likely something could go wrong—whether it's a robot navigating a warehouse or a drone scanning for wildfire hotspots. The Jetson Orin Nano Super thrives in these high-pressure environments because it eliminates one of the biggest bottlenecks in AI: latency.

Traditional AI systems depend on cloud computing—sending data to a remote server, waiting for analysis, and then receiving the result. That delay, while tolerable in some cases, is unacceptable when real-time decisions are required. The Orin Nano Super, on the other hand, processes information right where it's needed—at the edge. No waiting. No round trips. Just lightning-fast intelligence.

Take an autonomous delivery robot zipping through a hospital, navigating hallways full of people, carts, and equipment. If it had to wait for cloud instructions, it could easily crash or freeze. But with edge AI powered by the Jetson Orin Nano Super, it can respond instantly, ensuring smooth operation and safety.

This edge-first approach is also critical in areas with poor or unreliable connectivity.

Devices can keep working, even when the cloud goes dark. That makes the Orin Nano Super a perfect choice for remote environments, disaster zones, and mobile platforms.

What's more, by pushing workloads to the edge, we reduce the strain on central cloud infrastructure. As global data volumes continue to explode, distributing the workload through devices like the Jetson Orin Nano Super ensures a smarter, more scalable AI ecosystem.

Performance on a Budget: Smart Tech Without the High Price Tag

AI has traditionally been a luxury—one reserved for tech giants and institutions with massive budgets. But the Jetson Orin Nano Super flips that script by offering top-tier AI performance in a low-power, cost-effective package.

Operating at just 7 to 15 watts, this chip is a marvel of energy efficiency. That means it can power up drones, mobile robots, and portable devices without guzzling battery life. And compared to cloud-based systems that require massive energy to transmit and process data, the Orin Nano Super's local processing drastically reduces power consumption. This not only saves energy but is also kinder to the planet.

And let's talk about money. Every time you stream high-res video to the cloud for analysis, you're burning through bandwidth—and your budget. With the Jetson Orin Nano Super, all that processing happens on-device, eliminating those ongoing cloud costs.

Startups, researchers, and indie developers finally have access to powerful AI without needing a server farm or deep pockets. A small robotics company can build a fleet of AI-powered bots without footing the bill for cloud infrastructure. A rural clinic can deploy a diagnostic tool without relying on high-speed internet. This is how AI becomes affordable, scalable, and sustainable.

Power to the People: The Democratization of AI

Perhaps the most exciting impact of the Jetson Orin Nano Super is its role in democratizing AI—breaking down barriers and making cutting-edge technology available to everyone, not just the privileged few.

In the past, developing and deploying AI required vast resources, elite talent, and specialized infrastructure. But the Orin Nano Super levels the playing field. Its compact size, affordable price, and user-friendly development tools mean that anyone—from a student in a dorm room to a small-town engineer—can build intelligent systems.

The real magic lies in the ecosystem surrounding the chip. Tools like NVIDIA JetPack SDK and TensorRT give developers a plug-and-play experience with deep learning, computer vision, and high-performance inference—all without needing to write custom code from scratch. With a rich library of resources, documentation, and community support, the barriers to entry are lower than ever.

Researchers can now prototype and test ideas in the real world, not just in simulations. Startups can scale solutions from a single device to entire fleets. Educational institutions can teach the next generation of AI developers with hands-on tools that mirror professional-grade platforms.

This accessibility fosters innovation from all corners of the world. It's no longer just Silicon Valley pushing the frontier—it's students in Kenya building health monitors, scientists in Brazil automating crop management, and entrepreneurs in India solving urban traffic problems. The Jetson Orin Nano Super is the bridge that brings their ideas to life.

Chapter 5: The Future of Edge AI

A New Horizon with NVIDIA

The journey of edge AI is just beginning, and the future promises to be even more exciting. As technologies like the Jetson Orin Nano Super continue to push the boundaries of what's possible, we stand at the brink of a new era in artificial intelligence. But what does that future look like, and how will NVIDIA's leadership in edge computing guide us there? In this chapter, we explore the vision for edge AI, the challenges on the horizon, and what comes next in the evolution of this transformative technology.

The Vision for Edge AI: Smarter, Faster, and Everywhere

As we look ahead, the potential for Edge AI is practically limitless. Devices like the Jetson Orin Nano Super are already revolutionizing industries, enabling autonomous machines, smarter cities, and healthcare innovations. But the future is about scaling that intelligence across every corner of society—from smart factories to agriculture, healthcare to entertainment.

In the coming years, we can expect fully autonomous factories where machines don't just perform tasks—they adapt and optimize in real time. Robots on production lines will learn from their environment, adjust workflows dynamically, and collaborate with human workers seamlessly. Rather than relying on constant cloud processing, these systems will be entirely self-sufficient at the edge, capable of processing data on-site to make split-second decisions that drive efficiency and reduce downtime.

Agriculture is another sector on the verge of a major transformation. As the world's population grows and climate change continues to impact global food production, Edge AI will help farmers feed the world more sustainably. By embedding AI in drones and sensors, we will see real-time monitoring of crop health, predictive weather analytics, and precision farming practices that reduce waste and improve resource management. These devices will not only detect disease or pests but predict crop yields, enabling more sustainable farming practices.

In **healthcare**, the next generation of medical devices will be connected and intelligent, capable of real-time diagnostics, personalized treatment, and predictive analytics—all processed locally at the edge. Portable imaging systems will allow doctors in remote locations to perform high-level diagnostics without relying on expensive equipment or cloud infrastructure. This could lead to a more equitable healthcare system, with advanced technologies available even in the most underserved areas.

But the future of Edge AI isn't just about individual industries—it's about creating interconnected, intelligent systems that work together to solve global challenges. Smart infrastructure, for example, could automatically adjust energy consumption, optimize traffic flow, or monitor air quality, all while being powered by Edge AI devices that process data instantly and locally.

Upcoming Challenges: Scaling, Securing, and Standardizing Edge AI

While the future of Edge AI looks bright, it's not without its challenges. As the technology continues to grow, several obstacles will need to be addressed to ensure its widespread adoption and success.

Scalability will be one of the first hurdles. As more and more edge devices are deployed, there will be a need for seamless integration and interoperability. Devices from different manufacturers will need to work together efficiently, and standards must be developed to ensure that edge devices communicate and process data in a consistent manner. The challenge is to create a unified system that enables a wide variety of edge devices to operate as part of a cohesive network, without creating fragmentation or silos.

Security is another critical issue. The more devices that are connected at the edge, the more potential points of vulnerability there are. Data privacy and integrity will be of paramount concern, especially in industries like healthcare, finance, and transportation. Edge devices need to be secure from cyberattacks and data breaches, with robust encryption, secure boot mechanisms, and real-time threat detection capabilities. As Edge AI moves into industries with sensitive data, security will be an ongoing challenge that requires constant innovation.

Ethical concerns around AI also need to be addressed. As devices become more autonomous and capable of making decisions, questions of accountability, fairness, and bias arise. How do we ensure that AI-powered surveillance systems respect privacy rights? How do we ensure that autonomous vehicles make ethical choices in life-or-death situations? These are complex ethical dilemmas that will need to be tackled collaboratively by technologists, policymakers, and ethicists alike.

NVIDIA's Roadmap: Leading the Edge AI Revolution

As a pioneer in the world of AI and edge computing, NVIDIA is uniquely positioned to lead the charge into the next frontier of innovation. With a proven track record of creating high-performance hardware and software ecosystems, the company has already set the stage for the future of Edge AI—but it's only just beginning.

Looking ahead, we can expect even more powerful Edge AI chips from NVIDIA. The Jetson Orin Nano Super is already a marvel of engineering, but future iterations will continue to push the limits of what's possible, offering even greater computational power, memory capacity, and energy efficiency. These advancements will open up new possibilities for AI models that are more complex and capable of handling an even wider range of tasks.

In addition to hardware advancements, NVIDIA is likely to focus on developing specialized AI ecosystems for various industries. For example, Jetson might offer more tailored tools for autonomous vehicles, robotics, or smart cities, streamlining development for specific use cases. This industry-focused approach will make it even easier for developers to deploy AI solutions and accelerate innovation in their fields.

Emerging technologies will also play a key role in NVIDIA's roadmap. 5G is a natural partner for Edge AI, as the low-latency and high-bandwidth capabilities of 5G networks will complement the real-time processing power of edge devices. We could see exciting new applications in remote healthcare, autonomous transportation, and smart cities—enabled by the combination of 5G, Edge AI, and NVIDIA's platform.

As Edge AI continues to grow, NVIDIA is also committed to addressing the challenges of scalability, security, and ethics. By establishing standards for edge computing and ensuring its hardware is built with robust security features, NVIDIA will be a driving force in shaping the responsible and sustainable development of edge AI.

Chapter 6: Tales of Transformation

How the Jetson Orin Nano Super is Empowering Innovation

Innovation isn't just a buzzword—it's a driving force, propelling new ideas from concept to reality, often in the most unexpected ways. The Jetson Orin Nano Super is not just a chip; it's a platform that is enabling real-world breakthroughs, changing industries, and empowering the next generation of creators. In this chapter, we explore inspiring case studies that highlight the incredible potential of Edge AI.

These stories showcase how developers, researchers, and organizations are using the Jetson Orin Nano Super to solve complex problems, push technological boundaries, and improve lives in ways we never thought possible.

Saving Lives with AI-Powered Drones – A Lifeline in Crisis

When disaster strikes, every second counts. Time is a critical factor in rescue operations, and in many cases, human teams can't get to the scene fast enough to make a difference. AI-powered drones, equipped with the Jetson Orin Nano Super, have become an essential tool in modern-day rescue missions, providing an efficient and precise response when it matters most.

One compelling example comes from a global humanitarian organization that deployed AI-driven drones during a recent hurricane. In flood-affected areas, traditional rescue efforts were hindered by debris and waterlogged terrain. The drones, using real-time video analysis powered by the Jetson Orin Nano Super, were able to quickly pinpoint survivors, identify accessible routes for rescue teams, and map out damage—all in minutes.

This AI-powered response was far more efficient than human teams could have been in such difficult conditions, saving crucial time and potentially lives. The Jetson Orin Nano Super provided the computational power needed to make critical decisions on the fly, demonstrating the power of edge AI in disaster response.

Revolutionizing Agriculture – Smart Farming for a Sustainable Future

Agriculture is one of the most important industries worldwide, and yet it is under immense pressure to meet the demands of a growing population while minimizing environmental impact. Enter the world of precision farming, where AI-powered tools are transforming the way crops are grown, monitored, and harvested. The Jetson Orin Nano Super is enabling small-scale and industrial farmers alike to use cutting-edge technology that increases productivity and reduces waste.

One startup used the Jetson Orin Nano Super to develop a fleet of autonomous farming drones designed to monitor large crop fields. Equipped with AI models capable of identifying early signs of disease, pests, or soil imbalances, these drones can provide farmers with precise insights in real time. Instead of applying chemicals across entire fields, farmers can now target only the areas that need attention, reducing waste and minimizing environmental damage.

Another exciting application is the use of ground-based robots powered by the Jetson Orin Nano Super to autonomously harvest crops. These robots can navigate fields, identify ripe produce, and pick crops with precision, dramatically improving harvesting efficiency. By reducing human labor and increasing efficiency, these AI-powered machines are paving the way for more sustainable and profitable farming.

Environmental Monitoring – Protecting Our Planet with Real-Time Data

As the world grapples with climate change, environmental monitoring has become more important than ever. The Jetson Orin Nano Super is playing a key role in the fight against environmental degradation by enabling real-time data collection and analysis in remote and urban areas alike.

One innovative project used the Orin Nano Super to build a network of smart sensors that monitor air quality in urban areas. These sensors, equipped with AI models, can detect pollutants in real time, enabling authorities to take immediate action when pollution levels exceed safe thresholds. The system not only helps reduce exposure to harmful chemicals but also allows cities to make informed decisions about resource allocation and policy-making.

These smart sensors can also be deployed in natural disaster zones, helping monitor conditions like temperature, humidity, and soil moisture. In flood-prone areas, for example, the sensors can detect rising water levels and send early warnings to local authorities, giving them valuable time to evacuate residents and mitigate damage. The Jetson Orin Nano Super enables these devices to process data quickly on-site, eliminating delays associated with cloud processing and ensuring timely responses.

Enhancing Mobility – AI for Smarter, Safer Cities

Smart mobility is becoming a key focus for cities around the world, aiming to improve transportation efficiency and reduce congestion. By integrating Edge AI with connected infrastructure, cities are using the Jetson Orin Nano Super to create real-time traffic management systems that adapt to changing conditions on the fly.

For instance, smart traffic lights powered by the Jetson Orin Nano Super analyze traffic flow and adjust light timing accordingly, reducing congestion and cutting down on fuel consumption. These systems can also identify accidents, detect traffic violations, and reroute vehicles in case of road closures, improving safety and reducing travel time for commuters.

Public transportation systems are also benefiting from Edge AI. In one project, autonomous buses powered by the Jetson Orin Nano Super are being used to transport passengers in controlled, urban environments. The buses use AI to navigate routes, avoid obstacles, and optimize stops, offering a glimpse into the future of smart, eco-friendly transportation.

Developer Perspectives – Innovators Share Their Stories

Behind every breakthrough powered by the Jetson Orin Nano Super are developers, engineers, and researchers who have used this powerful platform to turn their ideas into reality. Their stories highlight the versatility of the device and how it empowers them to tackle some of the world's most pressing challenges.

One developer in the robotics field shared how the Jetson Orin Nano Super enabled their team to create an autonomous navigation system that works in real-world environments. "Before the Orin Nano Super, we had to choose between performance and portability," they said. "With this platform, we don't have to compromise anymore. It gives us both the power we need and the flexibility to innovate."

Another developer working on environmental monitoring projects echoed similar sentiments. Their team used the Jetson Orin Nano Super to deploy a network of smart sensors for real-time air quality analysis. "The ability to deploy AI directly onto devices was a game-changer," they said. "It allowed us to deliver accurate insights instantly, without relying on cloud infrastructure."

For startups with limited resources, the Jetson Orin Nano Super is a game-changer. One entrepreneur working on AI-powered logistics described how this affordable platform helped them build an innovative system without breaking the bank. "NVIDIA's tools and documentation made it possible for us to build something incredible," they said. "With the Jetson Orin Nano Super, we were able to hit the ground running and get our solution to market faster."

Empowering the Next Wave of Innovation

The Jetson Orin Nano Super is more than just a tool; it's a catalyst for change. It's empowering people from all walks of life to bring their ideas to life, whether they're tackling global challenges, creating new industries, or improving everyday life. These stories of innovation are just the beginning. As more developers embrace

Edge AI, the potential for breakthroughs grows exponentially, transforming industries, economies, and societies.

Conclusion:

Embracing the Future of Edge AI

As we stand on the precipice of a new technological frontier, it's clear that Edge AI is not just a passing trend—it's the foundation of the future. The Jetson Orin Nano Super has proven itself to be more than a powerful chip; it's a catalyst that's unlocking new possibilities across industries and empowering creators, innovators, and problem-solvers to reimagine what's possible.

From autonomous robots in factories to AI-powered drones saving lives in disaster zones, the Jetson Orin Nano Super is enabling a world where technology works smarter, faster, and more efficiently, right at the edge of the network. It's a world where data doesn't have to travel long distances to be useful—it's processed, analyzed, and acted upon immediately, in the places where decisions matter most.

The Jetson Orin Nano Super is a symbol of what happens when cutting-edge technology is made accessible to everyone, from researchers and startups to large enterprises and everyday innovators. By democratizing AI, NVIDIA has made it possible for anyone with a vision to harness the power of artificial intelligence, regardless of size or scale. This shift is not just about providing tools—it's about creating opportunities for a broader group of people to participate in the AI revolution.

Looking to the future, the potential for Edge AI is boundless. As the technology continues to evolve, we can expect smarter cities, more efficient manufacturing, better healthcare solutions, and more sustainable agricultural practices—all driven by real-time intelligence. Edge AI is changing the way we think about computing, transforming industries, and improving lives in ways we never thought possible.

Yet, as we embrace these advancements, we must also be mindful of the challenges that lie ahead. From ensuring security and privacy to navigating ethical concerns and scalability issues, the future of Edge AI will require collaboration, innovation, and careful consideration. As the technology continues to advance, so too must our approach to its development and implementation.

Ultimately, the journey of Edge AI is just beginning, and with the Jetson Orin Nano Super leading the way, the possibilities are endless. Whether you're a developer, researcher, or entrepreneur, the future is filled with opportunities to create, innovate, and shape the world with intelligent systems that can adapt, learn, and act autonomously.

So, as you close this book, remember that the Jetson Orin Nano Super is more than just a piece of technology—it's a key to unlocking the future. A future where machines work in harmony with humans to solve the world's most pressing challenges.

A future where AI is not confined to the cloud, but is brought directly to the edge, where it can make a real difference.

The Jetson Orin Nano Super is your gateway to this future. The next chapter is yours to write.

Appendix:

Resources, Technical Details, and Further Exploration

As we conclude this journey through the world of Edge AI and the power of the Jetson Orin Nano Super, this appendix provides a curated set of resources, technical details, and next steps for those eager to dive deeper into this fascinating field. Whether you're an engineer, researcher, developer, or simply an enthusiast, the following resources will help guide your path forward as you explore the potential of Edge AI.

A. Technical Specifications of the Jetson Orin Nano Super

To better understand the raw power and capabilities of the Jetson Orin Nano Super, here are its key specifications:

- CPU Architecture: ARM Cortex-A78AE

- GPU: 512 CUDA cores based on NVIDIA Ampere architecture

- Tensor Cores: 16, optimized for deep learning and AI inference

- Memory: 4GB or 8GB LPDDR5 memory options

- Storage: 16GB eMMC storage (expandable with microSD)

- Performance: Up to 40 TOPS (Tera Operations Per Second)

- Power Consumption: 7W to 15W, depending on the workload

- Connectivity: Gigabit Ethernet, Wi-Fi (via module), Bluetooth

- I/O Ports: Multiple USB ports, GPIO pins, HDMI output, PCIe, and M.2

- Software: JetPack SDK, TensorRT for optimization, DeepStream for streaming analytics, CUDA, cuDNN, and more.

These specifications make the Jetson Orin Nano Super a compact yet incredibly powerful AI platform, capable of handling the most demanding edge AI applications in robotics, healthcare, smart cities, and more.

B. Getting Started with the Jetson Orin Nano Super

For those ready to jump into Edge AI development with the Jetson Orin Nano Super, the following steps will help you get started:

- Set Up Your Development Environment

- Install JetPack SDK, NVIDIA's comprehensive set of development tools.

- Follow Jetson Setup guides to set up your development environment, including connecting peripherals and ensuring your software is up-to-date.

- Explore the SDKs and Libraries

- Dive into TensorRT for optimized deep learning inference.

- Experiment with DeepStream SDK for building high-performance video analytics applications.

- Leverage CUDA for GPU-accelerated computing and parallel processing.

- Create Your First AI Application

- Start with pre-trained models for simple tasks such as image recognition or object detection.

- Utilize NVIDIA's Transfer Learning Toolkit to fine-tune models on your own datasets.

Build and deploy your first Edge AI application, experimenting with edge processing to analyze real-time data directly on the device.

Experiment with Edge AI Projects

- Try creating projects like autonomous vehicles, robotic arms, smart cameras, or drone applications.

- Utilize the Jetson Orin Nano Super's AI capabilities to make real-time decisions in environments such as robotics, healthcare, or agriculture.

- C. Learning and Development Resources

To deepen your understanding of Edge AI and the Jetson Orin Nano Super, check out these resources:

Books & Articles

- "Programming the NVIDIA Jetson Nano" by Dimitrios K. Zissis

- "AI at the Edge: Machine Learning on Embedded Systems" by Javier Fernández

Online Courses

- NVIDIA's Deep Learning Institute (DLI) offers hands-on, self-paced courses on machine learning, deep learning, and AI development tailored for the Jetson platform.

- Coursera offers courses in Edge AI, Machine Learning, and Robotics.

NVIDIA Developer Forums

- Join the NVIDIA Developer Forums to discuss projects, ask for help, or share ideas with fellow developers working on Jetson and Edge AI projects.

GitHub Repositories

Explore a wealth of community-driven projects and codebases on GitHub, where developers share their AI applications built with Jetson devices.

Official Documentation

Jetson Developer Docs provide extensive technical information, including how to install and configure software, optimize performance, and build custom AI solutions.

C. Edge AI Applications and Use Cases

Here are a few inspiring Edge AI applications that showcase the broad capabilities of the Jetson Orin Nano Super:

Autonomous Vehicles: AI-enabled edge devices that help self-driving cars interpret sensor data in real time for safer driving.

Healthcare Devices: Real-time patient monitoring systems powered by AI that provide instant diagnostics and alert medical professionals about emergencies.

Smart Cameras: AI-enhanced video surveillance systems that can detect suspicious behavior or monitor traffic flow in real time, all while reducing the reliance on cloud services.

Agricultural Drones: Autonomous drones equipped with AI to monitor crops, detect diseases, and optimize irrigation in real-time without human intervention.

Smart Cities: Edge AI systems embedded in city infrastructure to improve everything from waste management to traffic control, energy efficiency, and environmental monitoring.

D. The Road Ahead for Edge AI

As Edge AI continues to evolve, its impact will grow across every industry and region. The potential for real-time, local decision-making is limitless, and we are only scratching the surface of what's possible with devices like the Jetson Orin Nano Super.

The future of AI lies not in distant data centers but at the edge—on the devices and systems that shape our daily lives. With NVIDIA's leadership in edge computing and AI, the next wave of technological innovation will be faster, more efficient, and more intelligent than ever before.